JONATH

How To Survive
A
Zombie Apocalypse

Winner of
WriteForTheStage Prize
for New Writing 2018

WRITEFORTHESTAGE Books
Manchester
www.writeforthestage.co.uk

Copyright © 2019 J.Hall

All rights reserved.

ISBN: 9781790900756

Jonathan Hall has asserted his right to be identified as the author of this work.

All rights reserved.

How To Survive A Zombie Apocalypse was first published in 2019 by *WriteForTheStage Publishing* - a division of *Studio Salford WriteForTheStage courses*.

CAUTION All rights whatsoever in the play are strictly reserved. Requests to reproduce the text in the whole or in part should be addressed to the publisher.

Professional Rights, Amateur Rights, Fringe Rights, Education Rights are all available through *WriteForTheStage Publishing*.

Please email **info@writeforthestage.co.uk** to discuss this with us.

No performance of any kind may be given unless a licence has been obtained. Applications should be made before rehearsals begin.

Publication of this play does not necessarily indicate its availability for performance.

CONTENTS

HOW TO SURVIVE A ZOMBIE APOCALYPSE 1

NOTES FROM THE AUTHOR..........107

ABOUT THE AUTHOR 109

NOTES FROM THE PUBLISHER 110

PERFORM THIS PLAY 111

BE A PLAYWRIGHT.............................111

How To Survive A Zombie Apocalypse was first performed at Kings Arms Theatre 19th- 21st July, 2018 during The Greater Manchester Fringe Festival, 2018

Produced by Narthen Productions, with the following cast:

PHIL Tobias Christopher
MARK Lee Petcher

Director Andy Pilkington

Production Support Matthew Taylor, Emma Drysdale

CHARACTERS

PHIL, 52
PHIL, 29

The play is set in and around Todmorden, West Yorkshire and the Lake District

To Louise

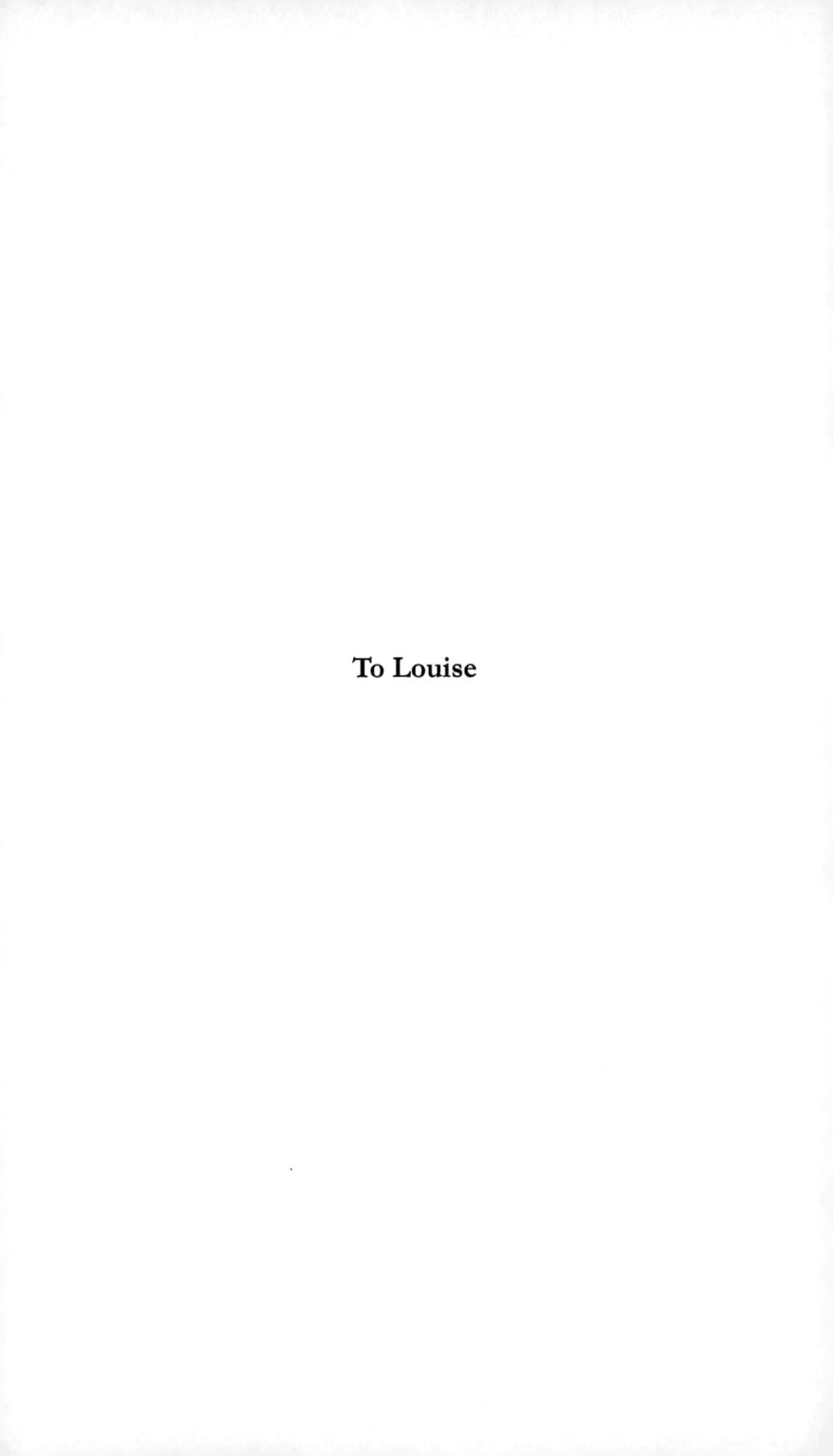

HOW TO SURVIVE A ZOMBIE APOCALYPSE

SCENE ONE

A four-metre pole, a ledge on the top.

PHIL, *wearing hard hat and harness is sat clinging to the ledge, eyes shut, trying to regain control of his breathing.*

MARK *appears beside him, below him, holding onto the pole.*

MARK You having fun there Sir?

PHIL *In an effort to be normal but with his eyes shut* I'm fine- it's fine-

MARK That's very true-

The reason being Animal's got you on 100% lock.

For you to fall, several very strong bits of heavy-duty nylon cable would

need to snap.

PHIL I just need a minute.

MARK There's no hurry whatsoever.

PAUSE

Okay- in a minute Sir-

When you're ready-

All I want you to do is stand up for me.

PHIL *opens his eyes.*

PHIL Shit.

MARK Looking down won't actually help-

All that'll do is make you think 'oh dear, I'm rather high up'.

PHIL Yes, I'm already doing that.

MARK You need to look at a fixed spot on the wall-

You're on 100 trillion percent lock.

PHIL What about the kids?

MARK The kids are fine-

They're getting kitted for the climbing with Pete and Jacs-

Which you **do not** have to do-

Look Sir, I'm going to climb up next to you-
Are you okay with that?

PHIL *nods*

Okay-

MARK *climbs onto the ledge.*

MARK Lovely day for a climb.

PHIL You must think I'm such a wimp.

MARK People get stuck up here all the time.

Now-

What I want you to do is just open your eyes but when you do keep them fixed on our rather shabby looking wall over there-

Just above the picture of the Little Mermaid.

PHIL *does so.*

That's very good-

Okay, now I'm going to stand up.

MARK *does so- puts his hand up.*

MARK Care to join me?

PHIL *gets half way- freezes, sits.*

MARK You're one hundred thousand million percent safe Sir-

Even if you did want to jump off, you aren't going anywhere.

These harnesses I'm reliably informed can hold a baby elephant-

And I know the Centre's pasties are good but even so.

But **PHIL** *doesn't move.*

MARK Look, can I ask-

You seem to be breathing a bit-

Do you have asthma?

PHIL One of the few things I don't have-

MARK That's great.

PHIL It's just being stuck at the top of a sixty-foot pole does things to your breathing.

MARK 4 metres actually.

PHIL Sorry?

MARK The trapeze pole.

About fourteen feet.

PHIL *suddenly stands, wobbles, falls and grabs at* **MARK**.

MARK Whoa- easy sir-

PHIL I'm sorry; I need to climb back down-

MARK Bit of a problem there Sir…

To do that you have to get your legs back under the ledge and find the footholds.

It's actually much much easier to just stand up and jump.

You don't even have to grab the trapeze.

PHIL I think we've different definitions of the word 'easy'.

MARK You'd be surprised what you can do.

PHIL You go climbing a lot?

MARK You are looking at an official bona fide rock face junkie-

Or you would be if you had your eyes open.

I go most weekends.

PHIL *opens his eyes.*

PHIL Shit-

MARK Look at the wall- look at the fixed point.

PHIL So this rock climbing- is this with what's her name?

MARK Michelle?

No- some lads from the Centre.

The Dow Crag Challenge.

PHIL And she's all right with it?

Michelle?

You going off every weekend?

MARK She's fine-

It's like okay-

You do your thing-

I'll do my thing-

We'll do our thing.

PHIL *stands, wobbles,* **MARK** *puts his arm around him.*

Steady-

Remember-

Animal's got you on lock.

PHIL Isn't it forecast to sile it down?

MARK I'm sorry?

PHIL This weekend- rock climbing.

MARK All part of it-

PHIL Being wet?

MARK There's this moment you get-

- when it's just you on the rock face-

And you get this feeling-

PHIL Like you're going to fall screaming to your death?

MARK Like- there's something there-

Something you've got to overcome.

PAUSE

PHIL I must seem so pathetic.

MARK Not a bit of it.

PHIL I just- froze up-

MARK You *stopped*.

PHIL I know I did.

MARK No, I mean you stopped and you thought about it.

Once you stopped and your brain kicked in and went 'hello- 4 metres above the ground'…

PHIL So the trick is not to stop.

MARK When I started climbing-

They taught us this trick-

Sing a song.

PHIL Sing a song?

MARK Sing a song.

PHIL 'And now the end is near'?

MARK … the momentum

- it keeps you going-

MARK *demonstrates marching.*

And I would walk five hundred miles
And I would walk five hundred more

Speaking

And up and on top and over.

PHIL Okay okay-

Just stop moving.

MARK I've stopped.

PHIL I'm just not cut out for this.

MARK Hey- I saw this film last night

With this group of people holed up after this disaster

And there was this one guy- not athletic in any way, shape or form

He walks across this narrow girder...

PHIL ...with only the camera crew and seventeen stuntmen to catch him.

MARK What I'm saying Sir-

- is we can all do things out of our comfort zone.

PHIL I know pretty well everything there is to know about comfort zones
Including how far out of the I can go.

MARK Okay let me ask you a question-

What about your walking holiday?

PHIL What walking holiday?

MARK ...the one you and your partner are off on- The hills of southern somewhere or other?

PHIL The hills of southern Dordogne.

MARK Sounded pretty full on to me- hills and vineyards.

PHIL It's a coach tour.

MARK Okay- a full on coach tour.

PHIL It is actually.

Calmer.

We both love it.

MARK Sounds great.

PHIL *slowly stands with his eyes shut.*

PHIL It is-

MARK Go for it-

PHIL's *eyes are still shut.*

PHIL All decisions taken out of your hands-

Except whether to drink red or white.

MARK Gently-

PHIL Sat out on some terrace-

Overlooking a valley of sunflowers-

Glass of the good vino-

The evening light.

MARK You can do it-

PHIL My two-week relaxation.

PHIL *is standing.*

PHIL *opens his eyes.*

MARK Don't sit down!

You can almost touch the trapeze-

Walk the girder Sir.

PHIL *on the edge of panic* So just what is this bit of inspirational cinema?

MARK Zombie Apocalypse 3: Dead Is The New Black.

PHIL I'm more Great British Bake Off.

MARK Look at the fixed point-

Come on- you can almost touch the trapeze.

PHIL *reaches for the trapeze- and then steps back.*

PHIL What do you say to one of the kids?
If they think they can't do something?

MARK You can do it.

Don't overthink it.

No one imposes limits but you yourself.

You **can** walk that girder.

PHIL No- **you** can walk that fucking girder-
I can tour the vineyards of southern France- in a bus.

PHIL *opens his eyes- and sits back down.*

LIGHTS DOWN

SCENE TWO

A park in Todmorden.

Early September.

PHIL- *wearing a suit and black tie- is sat on a bench, face turned up to the early autumn sunshine.*

MARK *enters carrying a shopping bag. Sees* **PHIL**.

MARK Hello Sir.

PHIL Mark.

MARK I thought it was you-

It's that whole weird thing isn't it?

When you see someone like out of context-

How's it all going, Sir?

PHIL I reckon you can probably drop the Sir.

MARK I'm sorry- work mode… delete delete.

PHIL How is work?

MARK Same old same old.

PHIL Need to get the ladder out for any more freaked out teachers?

MARK I told you.

It happens all the time.

Anyway- how was your terrace?

PHIL Sorry?

MARK The glass of good vino as the sun sets over the sunflowers.

PHIL You remembered-

MARK Kind of hard to forget.

PHIL It was very good.

MARK Yeah?

PHIL Us and a load of very game couples in pastel sweatshirts clutching Kath Kidston knapsacks.

Hey, ignore me, it was fine.

You're not working today?

MARK Afternoon off.

PHIL You've a nice day for it.

MARK I thought I'd take a run up Stoodley Pike later. That's the big one with the tower.

PHIL Literally a run?

MARK Maybe more a vigorous amble.

The view up there's amazing.

I'll just drop this lot off.

PHIL *gestures to the bag.*

PHIL What have you been buying?

MARK *opens the bag to show him.*

PHIL *takes out a water pistol*

PHIL Water pistols?

MARK Anti-zombie guns.

It's for Halloween.

I'm organising this Undead Party for the Centre staff.

PHIL You're big on the old zombies.

MARK We're going to barricade the managers and group leaders in the Archery courts and hammer on the doors moaning.

PHIL Excellent.

MARK So you not back at work? Schools round here started last week.

PHIL So did ours. I've the afternoon out.

PHIL *shows the black tie.*

MARK Oh- I'm sorry.

PHIL It's fine, don't worry about it.

MARK Was it -

PHIL - someone close?

MARK - if you don't mind me asking-

PHIL Someone I used to work with.

Celia

My classroom assistant.

Back in the day.

MARK Right-

PHIL I wouldn't say we were *close* close.

But I saw her everyday.

Suddenly-

Seven years had gone by.

Shit-

MARK What?

PHIL I've just worked it out-

It was twenty-five years ago.

Before you were born.

MARK I was four.

PHIL Just gives me a bit of a jolt when I realise I **have** a 'twenty five years ago' you know?

MARK Better to *have*, than *not* to have had a twenty-five years I'd say-

I saw this one film where they bumped everyone off at the age of 30-

PHIL 'Logan's run'.

MARK 'Logan's run'.

PHIL Michael York and Jenny Agutter.

MARK I'm sorry about your friend.

PHIL You really do think you'll go on forever.

MARK Death has a 1 in 1 success rate.

PHIL Cheers for that.

MARK I'm just saying- it comes to us all.

PHIL Some of us sooner than others.

MARK Come on.

PHIL I'm 52.

MARK You've got a few more years left I'd say.

PHIL Twenty maybe?

Not that long when you come to think about it.

3 series of 'Star Trek'-

Picard, Sisko, Janeway.

PHIL *mimes throat being cut.*

MARK That's cheerful.

PHIL You're the one big on the undead.

Think of it as a load of very still zombies-

You can fire on us with your anti zombie gun thingy-

Though when it's my turn I think I'll have mine full of chardonnay-

Anyway- here-.

PHIL *puts the gun back in the bag, sees what's inside.*

PHIL Those aren't anti zombie guns-.

MARK Clothes pegs.

PHIL So you can peg out your combat gear after decapitating the rampaging undead?

MARK I haven't got any.

PHIL Combat gear?

MARK Clothes pegs.

PHIL Didn't you say you'd been in your house for- what- 2 years?

MARK I have-

But the pegs-

They're Michelle's.

PHIL Are you not allowed to use them?

MARK That's sort of complicated.

PHIL You don't have to tell me.

MARK Thing is-

I mean it's no secret.

She's sort of moved out.

PHIL Sort of?

What- is she in the backyard?

Sorry.

MARK The term is 'We are officially on a break'.

PHIL I'm sorry.

MARK We're not over -

PHIL -you're just on a break-

MARK It's like we say.

Okay- we love each other-

That's the easy bit.

PHIL She's just moved out.

MARK We sort of want different things.

PHIL People who split up generally do.

MARK Except we've not actually split up.

PHIL Okay.

MARK I know, it gives me a headache. We just need a bit of time to 'get out heads together'

PHIL With each other or someone else?

Sorry, it's none of my business.

MARK There's no one else. It's just complicated.

Mexican 'Eese teeny bit complicated signor'

PHIL I hope it all works out for you.

MARK I believe the phrase is 'watch this space'.

PHIL There's always Dow Crag.

SILENCE

MARK *doesn't seem disposed to talk.*

PHIL I was thinking just now- sat here-

There's all the swallows on the wires -

Another summer gone.

MARK Yes indeedy.

PAUSE

PHIL How long were you-

-have you- been together?

If you don't mind me asking?

MARK Three years ... just over.

How about you?

You and-

PHIL -Patrick?

22… no, 23 years-

We got together just after I worked with Celia.

MARK I was six.

PHIL Luckily for Patrick I wasn't.

MARK It's an achievement though.

PHIL Certainly is-

MARK Why do you say it like that?

PHIL It's just people say that-

"well done"- like it's- I don't know

An allotment you've kept on top or something

And the truth is…it's something that… happens. Year in, year out.

Suddenly- 23 years have gone by.

MARK But you're both happy.

PHIL I know we are.

Semi in Baildon, flat screen TV.

Autumn Gold of the Loire Valley all booked for half term

MARK So?

PHIL No 'so' about it-

It's just… time passes

Puberty to prostate awareness, just like that-

You go on thinking things won't change

Not because they won't

Because it's easier to do so

Sorry-

Ignore me-

MARK People I work with right-

They keeping on saying stuff like- you know 'Soon be Friday'. And I always think it's like- they're wishing it all away, you know?

I want to say what's so good about Saturday or Sunday? How about making the most of Tuesday or Thursday.

PAUSE

But what do you do?

PHIL I know what **you** do-

- you go home and peg that washing out-

- and then you go and climb Stoodley Peak.

MARK Pike.

PHIL Pike.

MARK That sounds very much like a plan.

PHIL When you come to think about it- it must be quite straightforward with zombie apocalypse-

No fannying around with black ties or clothes pegs.

MARK There's this new one out meant to be rather epic-

'X, Y and Zee'.

PHIL You say 'new'-

MARK It's meant to be a totally different spin on the genre.

PHIL No zombies?

MARK Well **yes** of course zombies.

PHIL You need to see some of the old black and white classics

'The day the earth stood still'

'The day the earth caught fire'

'Village of the Damned'

PAUSE

Anyway

I need to be making tracks.

MARK *Suddenly* D'you fancy a swift half?

PHIL What about Stoodley Pike?

MARK It can wait half an hour.

PHIL Better not-

I need to let you get your washing pegged out.

MARK I suppose I better.

Take care Sir.

PHIL Mark-

MARK Yeah?

PHIL Drop the fucking Sir

They shake hands.

PHIL *is about to go but stops.*

PHIL Here

PHIL *hands him a card.*

MARK What's this?

PHIL If you ever fancy that swift half-

Talk serious sci-fi some time.

If the Lake District happens to be shut or something- Thursday nights are best.

MARK *suddenly nervous* Great.

PHIL It doesn't matter-

MARK What?

No, I'd like to-

I mean- I've a lot on at the moment.

But as soon as the dust settles.

PHIL 'Eese not a problem, Signor'

You take care.

I hope it all works out for you with everything.

As they say - 'have a nice life'

MARK You too Sir

PHIL *goes.*

MARK *looks at the number, stuffs it in his wallet.*

LIGHTS DOWN

SCENE THREE

Hebden Bridge Railway station, three weeks later.

PHIL *is offstage peeing.*

MARK Everyone?

PHIL *enters.*

PHIL Everyone.

Everything.

MARK That better?

PHIL -the whole village.

Spark out.

MARK Even the animals?

PHIL 'Midwich lay entranced.

While the rest of the world began to fill the day with clamour, Midwich slept on…

Its men and women,

Its horses, cows and sheep

Its pigs, its poultry

Its larks, moles and mice

All lay still.

MARK Presumably they all woke up at some point?

PHIL They did.

And when they did-

All the women of childbearing age… were pregnant.

MARK Shit.

PHIL -and the babies, when **they** were born- had white hair and golden eyes-

And they could make people do whatever they wanted them to.

MARK That'd suit Michelle.

Go on-

PHIL When John Wyndham was writing back in the 50's-

It was a pretty scary time.

People were terrified-

The Russians - the A bomb-

Everyone was convinced things were coming to an end.

MARK A bit like now-

PHIL I actually can't remember a time when people *didn't* think things were going pear shaped-

The Cold War… 9/11…Al Qaeda – Brexit-

MARK Every age has its' own apocalypse.

PHIL Even way back when- you had the plague. Witches being burnt.

MARK I bet you are a bloody good teacher.

PHIL I have my moments.

MARK You make it really interesting- "Sir".

PHIL Gets a bit harder when talking about possessive pronouns.

MARK So actually now- the way people are obsessed with zombies-

PHIL Communists, ISIS-

It's nothing new.

Just us with our little lives coming to terms with our own mortality.

MARK Okay now this is officially getting depressing-

PHIL Death is a fact of life-

MARK Again- slightly too miserable.

PHIL It's not miserable facing facts.

MARK Okay just maybe not on a Thursday night after a few beers.

PAUSE

Both seem content to just sit there.

PHIL The Autumn equinox.

MARK The what what?

PHIL September 23rd

The official start of the autumn.

PAUSE

MARK You're right though- when you come to think about it-

PHIL What?

MARK Time is short-

Picard, Sisko, Janeway-

What you said last time-

It was dead right.

Loads of people right- they just… bottle it.

There's this one guy I know…

He reckoned on how he'd always wanted to explore this one caving system in North Yorkshire-

Gordale scar-

Always going on about it-

When the chance came along to do it- what did he do?

PHIL Come to his senses?

MARK Cried off

Said he was full of cold.

PHIL Take a Lemsip and get a grip man.

MARK Exactly.

I'm never going to be like that.

PHIL You make Bear Grylls look like a couch potato-

MARK *laughs.*

They touch fists.

PHIL It's been a good night.

MARK I can talk to you.

They kiss.

They jump apart, the impulse is mutual.

PHIL Oh God Oh God-

MARK It's okay-

PHIL No, I'm sorry-

MARK It's fine-

PHIL It's my fault-

MARK Forget it

PAUSE

PHIL I wish I knew where that train's got to-

MARK Remember you're the other platform -

PHIL Yes-

MARK - the Leeds train, not the Brighouse one.

PHIL I know-

MARK Should be due along minute- I'll check my app.

PHIL Hang on-

MARK Two secs-

PHIL Let's just stop.

MARK I'm not with you.

PHIL Stop babbling on about trains.

MARK I wasn't aware that I was.

PHIL Post kiss babble.

MARK Actually I need a pee.

PHIL No, wait up a sec-

Look okay you're thinking-

Like I'm thinking-

Something along the lines of 'shit'.

MARK Actually I'm thinking I just need to pee.

PHIL And you're worried that –

I'm going to bombard you with texts

Or turn up at your house//

MARK Not really-

PHIL //or tell Michelle.

Or, I dunno-

- the ultimate Apocalypse scenario-

- me coming shooting down the Centre zip wire, trailing pink scarves like a very athletic Priscilla Queen of the Desert.

MARK No, really I'm not-

PHIL Look

I have kissed a fair number of men.

I know what I'm talking about.

And relax-

None of the above are going to happen.

Don't you need to pee?

MARK Okay- don't take this the wrong way-

I mean you're a sound bloke and all that-

It's just- well- I'm not gay.

PHIL I know.

MARK I mean I don't want to give you the wrong idea or anything.

PHIL Wrong idea not received

PAUSE

MARK That train's late-

PHIL Bottom line it was a good evening-

MARK Agreed-

PHIL A real laugh-

MARK Totally-

PHIL I learnt things about the whole zombie oeuvre I didn't know existed.

And- thing is Mark-

Well- okay- I'm 52, respectable Deputy Head-

And okay, face facts- I've just had a kiss on Hebden Bridge station-

Which is sort of great-

But-

Will I pester you? No.

Will I go home and say what I've done? Definitely no.

That's it-

That's as far as it goes-

That's where this particular zombie film ends.

Okay?

MARK Okay

PHIL Good.

MARK As I say I'm not even sure why it happened-

PHIL Five pints of Theakstons?

They smile. **MARK** *goes off to pee.*

PHIL Why are men so *shit* with kissing?

MARK *Offstage* Hardly kissing-

PHIL This one guy I met-

I went to kiss him- and he says 'I don't do weird stuff'-

MARK Like I say-

'Me no gay Signor'.

PHIL Look on it as a one off.

A new experience.

I dunno- like white water rafting.

MARK *Entering* And-the fact is- I really do love Michelle.

PHIL I know.

And that's good.

MARK It would be if we were together-

PAUSE

PHIL I remember the night when I kissed the man I knew I'd spend the rest of my life with-

MARK So where did you meet Patrick?

PHIL This wasn't Patrick-

It was someone I never saw again

Except at a distance-

In IKEA-

With what presumably were his wife and kids.

MARK Ouch.

PHIL No, the first time I kissed *Patrick*- I said don't get any ideas; this is strictly a one off.

MARK But you love him.

PHIL Yes.

MARK Of course you do.

PHIL Sorry, did I sound like I didn't?

Sorry, that 'yes' was a 22 years- mortgage- cancer scare- coach holidays- 'yes'.

PAUSE

You'll sort it with Michelle if you want to-

PAUSE

It's such a clear night-

MARK I can't actually see life without her-

PHIL So get in touch-

MARK No easy signor.

PHIL Pick up the phone-

MARK It's just -

PHIL - complicated Signor?

I tell you something- one of the very very few good things about getting older-

You realise all these various apocalypses you and everyone else was freaked out by back in the day-

You know… rabies- mad cow disease- AIDs- SARs- Bird 'flu- Ebola- that Zika…thing.

These scary nightmare scenarios didn't come to pass-

Not in the way the Daily Mail would have us believe.

MARK She wants kids.

PHIL And you don't?

MARK No-

PHIL Not now?

MARK No-

PHIL Later?

MARK No.

I don't know

PAUSE

PHIL See that star- above the trees- the bright one.

MARK To the right of that chimney?

PHIL That's Alioth-

Brightest star of the plough.

81 light years away.

You're looking at that star as it was 81 years ago.

MARK 81 years.

PHIL That's how long it took the light to travel here.

In 81 years time none of this will matter.

We'll all be dead and gone.

MARK Right.

PHIL Don't you find that comforting?

MARK No.

PAUSE

Maybe.

Noise of a train siren.

PHIL That's me.

Puts out his hand. They realise they've both peed and think better of it.

MARK A good night Sir.

PHIL We should do this again.

MARK *Over hearty meaning 'I'm not sure'* Indeedy-

PHIL Relax.

I'm too old to be lead up any garden paths.

LIGHTS DOWN

SCENE FOUR

Three weeks later.

The top of Stoodley Pike.

MARK *strides on, full of energy.*

MARK So it was all rather interesting right… there I was-

Upside down in wet mud

And I'm thinking- I can't actually move here-

Flings himself down to take in the view.

PHIL *enters, out of breath.*

MARK *gets out his phone.*

MARK Here's the entrance to the caves-

There's Animal stood next to them-

You get a sense of the sheer **scale** of the place-

PHIL With all this caving and rock climbing do you not ever get sick of just like walking?

He is rubbing his foot.

MARK Frequently.

At the risk of doing my broken record impression-

You could do with getting some proper boots.

PHIL I've got some.

MARK I thought you said you didn't have any.

PHIL I didn't.

I do now. Since the last time I saw you.

Just like I used to use.

MARK You could have done with them today-

PHIL Had I had any idea we were doing an episode of Bear Grylls challenge would have.

MARK It's only Stoodley Pike

PHIL 'How about a drink' your text said-

MARK We can head back down.

PHIL We've only just got here.

MARK *getting up* You're the one wanting a drink.

PHIL Hang on a sec.

Tell me about this view.

Where am I looking at?

MARK Over there- right across the valley-

There's the Centre.

And across there- that's Penistone.

Over that way; that's Heptonstall.

PHIL It's lovely-

MARK When you think about it-

You spend so much of your life in *rooms*.

Schools - offices- gyms-

PHIL A & E.

MARK I like to come up here when I'm pissed off.

PHIL And are you?

MARK What?

PHIL Pissed off?

MARK No.

Jumps up.

How's Patrick?

PHIL Currently away with Chamber abusing his liver in some Brexit hotspot.

MARK Did you ever get him to the gym?

PHIL Watch this space.

MARK Is he any healthier?

PHIL At the outlet mall-

When we were getting the boots-

Three times he had to sit down.

I swear his breathing's getting worse-

MARK Lead by example-

PHIL Thank you.

It was a surprise- when you texted.

MARK Was it?

PHIL It'd been over three weeks.

MARK You could've texted me.

PHIL I could-

MARK When did you climb?

PHIL Climb what?

MARK 'Just like I used to use'

PHIL Years ago- pre Patrick.

MARK Which fells?

PHIL I don't know-

Steep ones-

The Three Peaks.

Kinder Scout.

The Old Man of Coniston.

MARK 2,634 feet.

PHIL Now I just *am* the Old Man of Coniston.

MARK Damn, I've left my violin at home.

PHIL So how's Michelle dare I ask?

MARK Very well I think.

Seeing someone else.

PHIL Ah.

MARK But it's all good.

'eese fine Signor'-

He works in a bank.

PHIL A banker.

MARK A right banker by all accounts.

PHIL I'm sorry.

MARK I'm not.

Good luck to her.

PHIL And you are, presumably.

MARK I am what?

PHIL Seeing someone-

That *is* the remains of a love bite on your neck.

MARK *is rubbing at it.*

PHIL I don't think they come off.

MARK It's nothing-

Just something that happened.

PHIL Fair enough.

MARK Just one of the instructors- Mandy- nice girl. Just a bit of fun.

PHIL And was it?

MARK Was it what?

PHIL Fun.

MARK Not really.

You know what it's like. When some people… want more than you do.

PHIL Ah.

MARK - they can't see it for what it is.

PHIL And you don't want more?

MARK Not at the moment, no.

It's like the climbing wall.

PHIL Is it?

MARK Good for an afternoon. You just don't want to necessarily live there.

PHIL I didn't text on purpose.

MARK Okay.

PHIL Last time- it all got a bit weird.

MARK "Does not compute"-

I mean – no offence- like I said -it's not like I'm gay or anything-

Not that there's anything whatsoever wrong with being gay.

PHIL When I didn't hear from you- I thought- has he got the wrong idea?

Just don't … I don't want you to look on this like a zombie film.

MARK Okay that's random.

PHIL Zombie films-

They all follow a pattern:

Normality… normality shatters… apocalypse… battle for survival-

Life- **doesn't** follow neat set patterns.

I mean people want it to-

If you see someone, people think it's supposed to… follow a pattern- mean something.

MARK Not sure I'm 100% following this-

PHIL Like – we go out- talk science fiction-

Have a few beers.

A laugh.

MARK Totally.

PHIL That's **it**… End of story.

There's really no need whatsoever to charge me up hillsides in case I get heavy.

MARK The other night when I texted-

It was stupid really.

PHIL Oh?

MARK I was in the pub with people from work-

And we were talking about-

I don't know-

Some new canoes the Centre had bought or something.

And Jacs, she brought some smoky bacon crisps-

And she rips open the packet and puts it on the table and says 'dig in people'…

Like she always does.

And James he does his Darth Vader impression…

Like *he* always does.

And Animal- when it's his turn to get a round in…

He goes 'More tea Vicar'- like *he* always does.

And I thought- I actually know every single word these people are going to say

Like **how** many times have I heard this before?

I thought like- is this *it*?

Like- I'm nearly thirty-

PHIL I wish I was.

MARK I don't know.

I just need to get a grip and take a Lemsip.

PHIL We all get times when we wonder-you know- about life.

Everyone does.

Like that Saturday with Patrick-

Sitting there at the Castleford mall waiting for him to get his breath back

You think to yourself-

You start off with Heathcliff -you end up with Homer Simpson.

It doesn't mean you're not where you should be-

With the person you should be with.

MARK You know about yourself.

PHIL I do?

MARK Where you're going- what you're doing.

PHIL You think one day I'll have life sorted.

I remember when I was your age-

I used to think by the time I was fifty- I'd have life sorted.

Done, labeled, boxed off.

MARK Partner- house- sounds pretty sorted to me.

PHIL It'll happen to you and you'll see what I mean.

MARK I don't know if I want it to.

PHIL You can't spend all your life up Dow Crag.

MARK You watch me try!

PHIL I'm just resisting the impulse to throw my Crabtree and Evelyn loyalty card into the air and whoop

A smile. A moment.

MARK What I like about seeing you-

I like… not knowing what's coming next.

And that's not an invitation for anything in any way weird.

PHI Don't worry- I'm a bit old for anything weird.

MARK Can I ask you something?

PHIL I hate that.

MARK What?

PHIL When people say that-

'Can I ask you something?'

What they really mean is "Can I ask you something you're not going to like?"

Go on- ask away.

MARK Why do you keep saying that?

PHIL What?

MARK You're too old-

It's like your some sort of geriatric.

PHIL It's true.

MARK Not from where I'm standing.

PHIL Hadn't we better be getting back?

MARK There you go again-

"Better be getting back"

Why? Just what do you think'll happen if we don't Global catastrophe? The collapse of the banking system?

PHIL I rather think that's already happened.

Look - There's things you can do and things you can't do.

And maybe we only want to do the things we can't do because we know we can't do them.

MARK Why not though?

PHIL A hundred reasons.

MARK Like you're scared?

PHIL You get scared for a reason.

Scared you might fall off a cliff-

Scared the undead might rip out your throat.

MARK It doesn't mean you shouldn't do stuff.

PHIL Okay- so what do you think I should do?

MARK Easy- break your boots in.

PHIL I'm going to.

MARK Where?

PHIL I don't know- down the canal.

MARK You could walk that in flip-flops.

PHIL Okay: where do you suggest?

MARK Coniston Old Man. 2,634 feet

PHIL *Sighing* Right-

MARK What?

PHIL In your bloody dreams -

LIGHTS DOWN

SCENE FIVE

The noise of wind and rain, which keeps up throughout the following.

A bedroom in a B and B in Coniston.

MARK *is checking his phone.*

Noise of enormous piss offstage.

PHIL *offstage* What storm is it the remains of?

MARK Storm Phil?

PHIL Sorry? *Enters.* Any texts?

MARK Why would there be?

PHIL Look just so you know- this is not all some plan on my part.

MARK It's fine.

PHIL I mean you heard what she said- it's her last room.

MARK Not a problem.

PHIL Probably the last room in whole of Coniston. I'll sleep on the floor

PHIL *sits on the bed, winces and rubs his knee.*

MARK Which'll probably kill you.

PHIL *belches.*

MARK The brandy not work?

PHIL It's getting there.

I'll sleep in the chair.

MARK You could just hang out of the window by your fingertips.

It's fine- seriously.

Chill-

PHIL I am chilled.

Look, we really couldn't have slept in the tent.

MARK I say it'd have been okay.

PHIL Yeah, in what sense of the word 'okay' does sleeping halfway up mountain in a hurricane come under?

MARK The campsite's by the lake.

PHIL It'd have been **in** the lake by morning.

MARK Bigger picture Sir- you did it.

PHIL Yay.

MARK 2,634 feet.

Ping of a text.

PHIL Michelle? All right, I'm not asking.

We can always put pillows down the middle

MARK It's a bed not bloody Guantanamo bay.

Goes into the bathroom.

PHIL In terms of a bathroom it's more like something Superman would get changed in.

Throughout the following **PHIL** *putting on pyjamas and dressing gown as* **MARK** *talks to him from offstage.*

MARK A good day Sir.

PHIL A bit on the wet side.

MARK I told you you could do it.

PHIL Often.

MARK It's like I was saying in the pub

It's about actually … *doing* it-

Thinking I **can** do this.

PHIL I nearly gave up.

MARK Even if it does mean you're slightly out of your comfort zone.

PHIL I've forgotten what a comfort zone is.

MARK *singing* And I will walk five hundred miles

And I will walk five hundred more-

PHIL Is that you or the Hawkshead lager?

MARK We got to the top!

PHIL With all that mist it might as well have been the bloody car park.

MARK It's about seeing where your boundaries are

Testing them-

Trying something new

MARK *enters in his boxers.*

PHIL *by now buttoned up to the nines in pyjamas and dressing gown is slightly thrown by this.*

PHIL You want to watch TV?

MARK I'm good.

PHIL Catch the local weather?

MARK I checked earlier on my phone.

PHIL Okay so where did we go again?

MARK *produces the map, which he opens with some drunken faff.*

MARK We started here-

We went up here- up this stream here-

PHIL Was that where we found the dead sheep?

MARK No- that was a bit further on- here.

PHIL Where was that really heavy downpour?
Where we had to shelter under that plastic sack?

MARK Here-
And here's the top.

PHIL 2,634 feet.

MARK 2,634 feet.

PHIL I actually did it-

MARK You certainly did.

PHIL That moment, when we got to the cairn-

And I realised it was the top-

It was... brilliant.

Thank you.

MARK You're very welcome.

PAUSE

Another beer Sir?

PHIL Better not-

You go ahead.

MARK I'm good.

PHIL Actually I reckon I'll turn in.

MARK Okay.

PHIL -I mean you read- or watch TV if you want-

There maybe some late night zombies.

MARK I'm good.

PHIL Of course you could call Michelle-

All right- I know I promised not to say anything-

But she did text you.

Okay- I'll shut up.

Night.

MARK Eeese good day Signor

A clumsy handshake that could have been a hug.

They get into bed.

PAUSE

MARK And I would walk five hundred miles and I would walk five hundred more.

We could maybe walk round the lake tomorrow.

PHIL I probably need to be getting back.

MARK Not a problem.

PHIL Night.

MARK Night-

PAUSE

MARK I know what I meant to tell you.

PHIL Sorry?

MARK I saw some of what you earthlings call – homoerotica.

PHIL Mmm?

MARK Some free channel.

I was doing a bit of the old channel hopping… As you do.

PHIL You watched gay porn?

MARK Not *watched* watched-

PHIL Bear Grylls not on?

MARK Mighty strange habits you folk have-

PHIL It's not real.

MARK Looked real enough to me.

PHIL Well it's not like that.

MARK Like what?

PHIL Like whatever it was you saw.

MARK So in what way is it not real?

PHIL You and Michelle-

That was like straight porn?

MARK Sometimes-

The old Planet Boff off.

PHIL The old planet what?

MARK You know- when you're having a bit of fun.

PHIL What? You stop in the middle and play Ludo?

MARK So what about you and Patrick?

PHIL What about us?

MARK If you don't mind me asking?

I mean tell me to shut up.

PHIL Shut up.

Anyway, there's nothing to ask about-

MARK Oh?

PHIL We're like any other couple that's been together 20 plus years.

MARK Earth calling Philip. Does not compute.

PHIL Some homophobe once said to me-

'It's not who you are… it's what you do I can't get my head round'-

I said what's that?

Argue in Asda?

Because that's about it.

MARK So you're saying… that you and Patrick… don't do stuff any more?

PHIL If you're talking in terms of the Planet Boff Off -

The rocket's gone rusty.

MARK The Earthman methinks he joketh.

PHIL The Earthman he doesn't-

I'm serious

MARK Okay

PHIL The other week-

We were in bed-

Suddenly there's all this huffing and puffing.

I thought 'shit, what's this?'

Turns out he was having an asthma attack.

Anyway

PHIL *turns away, as far as he's concerned the conversation is over.*

MARK So have you ever thought of- tell me to shut up.

PHIL What?

MARK Like going and seeing someone?

PHIL A threesome?

MARK Like a therapist.

PHIL A therapist?

MARK Like a Counselor.

PHIL And say what exactly?

MARK You know- what is and is not happening.

PHIL Good afternoon Doctor. I've been with my partner 22 years and we no longer have sex. 'Next!'.

MARK If it matters surely?

PHIL Who said it matters?

I mean… I suppose it's a bit sad

But only if I stop to think about it.

You get to a point where...

I don't know- it's had its day.

MARK Had its day?

PHIL That's why I reckon people like porn. We all love the idea that the world is full of buffed car mechanics and cute pizza delivery boys all set to squirt us with oil and lick our nadgers.

Reality's just not like that.

PHIL *Turns over, as far as he's concerned the conversation is definitely over.*

PAUSE

MARK Can I ask you another question?

PHIL What if I said 'no'?

MARK Sorry.

PAUSE

PHIL Go on.

MARK It's just – I've always been a bit- curious-

What did you do? When you do it- did it- with anyone?

PHIL Did you not see on the Homo Channel?

MARK You said that wasn't real.

PHIL It's not like with a man and a woman.

Like with a man and a woman- climbing boots- cliff face-

Natural match.

With two men- climbing boot- climbing boot.

MARK Did anyone ever tell you- you are mad?

PHIL Bits are left over.

MARK You think that's why they all use so much stuff?

PHIL Stuff?

MARK On this channel - these guys…

There was all this **stuff**-

These *chains*

And there were all these – it looked like black plastic bin bags –

I take less to the climbing wall-

PHIL Nipple clamps?

MARK Seriously?

PHIL Piercings?

MARK I've heard of that.

PHIL This one guy I went out with-

Heavily into piercings- you know- down there.

MARK Ouch.

PHIL...foreplay used to sound like the opening bars of 'jingle bells'.

MARK You are mad- 'eese official'.

PHIL That's what I realised climbing that last hill.

MARK So basically what you are saying is sex between two men is crap.

PHIL Not crap- just not all it's cracked up to be.

MARK I just always thought-

PHIL What?

MARK It doesn't matter.

PHIL Go on.

MARK It could be like- I don't know- uncomplicated.

PHIL No strings?

MARK Just two people-

PHIL We're back to the climbing wall are we?

MARK *goes to kiss him, but* **PHIL** *moves back.*

MARK Shit- sorry-

PHIL No, I'm sorry, it's me-

MARK I'm sorry, it's my fault-

PHIL Stop a sec.

MARK It's okay, just leave it.

PHIL Listen-

MARK What?

PHIL Look …it's just- there's you- 30-

MARK 29.

PHIL You're up that climbing wall every verse end-

And- there's me.

MARK What about you?

PHIL I'm 52-

MARK So what

PHIL So look-

PHIL *gets out of bed, opens his pyjama top.*

PHIL Look-

Look at me-

I keep saying I'm going to join a gym

I haven't seen my abs in years-

And here-

That's where they took out my gallbladder-

And here- missing teeth

And if you put your ear to here you can listen to the steak'n'ale pie fighting the - Gaviscon. *Sits back down.*

MARK It's just a bit of fun-

PHIL *doesn't look up.*

MARK Gordale scar right-

You go down it to get to the caves-

There's these marks on the side

Where the waters been

Where trees have grown

Different layers of rock

Runs his fingers down **PHIL'S** *chest.*

The marks of time they call it

Kisses him.

It's – kind of lovely.

PHIL You are so full of crap.

MARK No strings-

PHIL Climbing wall it is.

They kiss again and the lights dim.

SFX I will walk 500 miles.

LIGHTS DOWN

SCENE SIX

The next day.

MARK's *house.*

A tip. Pizza boxes everywhere.

PHIL *is on the phone.*

MARK *comes in with his rucksack from the weekend.*

PHIL *Covering the phone* Did you get your walking socks?

MARK *silently holds up a pair of sodden muddy socks.*

PHIL Sorry… yes, the address-

MARK 12, Calder Terrace.

PHIL 12 Calder Terrace.

MARK The one straight after the viaduct.

PHIL The one straight after the viaduct.

Yes.

Have you any idea about how long?

Sorry?

Look- is there any chance of making it any sooner?

It's just I have to get home?

Of course-

I understand-

Thanks.

PHIL *rings off.*

About an hour-

MARK Okay.

PHIL They might come quicker but the mechanics the far side of Halifax on another job.

Listen I can go and wait in a café or something; they've got my number.

MARK It's fine.

PHIL You were wanting to get off to the climbing wall.

MARK It's reet *(Meaning 'it's all right')*

Do you want a brew?

I've no milk- at least none that's not- *does Twilight Zone music*

PHIL I'm good thanks.

PAUSE

MARK I was meaning to have a tidy round before I went away.

PHIL I should buy shares in your pizza place.

MARK Oh- ha ha.

PHIL Do you have- is there any heat?

MARK Oh- yes- sorry.

I turned it off as I wasn't going to be here.

MARK *turns it on*

PAUSE

MARK Are you sure about the tea?

PHIL Have you any herbal?

MARK *looks at him*

PHIL It's okay.

PAUSE

This is the first time I've come back from a dirty weekend actually dirty-

Sorry-

PAUSE

Look, I'm sorry.

MARK What for?

PHIL Me.

How I'm being-

How I was on the way back in the car-

Mr. Miserable Git-

It's really and truly nothing to do with you.

MARK I didn't think it was.

PHIL It's just… what happened.

MARK Do we need to go on about it?

PHIL Not that I didn't enjoy it-

But bottom line-

I shouldn't have done it- and I'm sorry.

MARK Not a big deal.

What happens in Coniston stays in Coniston.

PHIL At the end of the day, who likes someone who cheats on their partner?

MARK That'd only be a problem if someone were to find out-

No strings remember.

PHIL Just a bit of fun.

MARK If you like.

PHIL The all purpose male explanation-

Okay, my darling, I've been shagging away behind your back on a truly industrial scale but hey, guess what?

It was just a bit of fun-

MARK Look, do we actually need to keep going on about this?

PHIL What I'm not not **not** going to do is dress it up.

MARK Look-

PHIL 'I did it for me'…'Me time'…'what I did doesn't affect us'…

MARK Look: it happened.

Maybe it shouldn't have but at the end of the day it did. And the way I look at it you've got two choices

And you can either beat yourself up about it- or you can move on-

I'm not being funny but can we change the subject?

PAUSE

MARK And – bigger picture- Coniston Old Man- 2,634 feet.

PAUSE

They smile. Touch fists.

PHIL I think the heat's coming on.

PAUSE

MARK I've got to get round to getting this place sorted.

PHIL Are you any further on with getting a lodger?

MARK It just seems like an awful lot of hassle.

PHIL Nothing more from Michelle?

MARK No.

PHIL That text you got in the car?

Sorry-

I mean she still wants to see you?

MARK Indeedy.

PHIL And definitely it's all off with the banker?

MARK He is an ex banker, he has ceased to be.

PHIL So- look- sorry, this is none of my business-

But why *aren't* you meeting her?

If she wants to.

MARK What would be the point?

PHIL To see her.

MARK And what exactly?

PHIL Talk?

MARK We've talked.

We've talked till we're both various of shades of blue in the face.

Like I said to you last night-

I know how she feels-

She knows how I feel-

American The positions do not correlate commander.

PHIL And the thought of having a kid is so terrible?

MARK It's just not for me.

PHIL No more trolling off down Gordale Scar-

MARK It's really not that-
It's just-

PHIL- a scary thought?

MARK Yes.

PHIL This from the man who climbs sheer rock faces-

PAUSE

Patrick told me-

When he found out he was going to be a Dad-

He drove up on Baildon moor and cried his eyes out.

And now- he wouldn't be without them.

MARK Patrick has kids?

PHIL Didn't I say?

MARK No-

PHIL Hannah and Sarah. From before I met him of course.

MARK How old?

PHIL Hannah's 24- studying law.

And Sarah- she's 22- setting up her own plumbing business.

We reckon she's going to end up on 'The Apprentice'.

They both nag him to lose weight.

MARK And you all get on alright?

PHIL Fine.

I mean we've had our sticky moments-

But on the whole yes.

But what I'm saying with them-

I mean he thought when they came along
'This is it'

Life will never be the same again.

And he was right, it wasn't.

2 little beings that upskittle your world.

But he says- what he didn't realize was how much **better** life would be-

Family holidays- birthdays- school Nativity plays.

MARK I'm just not ready for all that.

PHIL I don't know if anyone ever *is-*

He winces.

MARK That knee again?

PHIL It seems to have stiffened up-

Along with the back- the neck - the elbow.

MARK Bloody crock.

PHIL I just love getting old.

MARK You're all right, I've a spare body bag in the back.

I said you should get it seen to properly.
By a sports therapist- there's one comes to the Centre.

PHIL Just wake me up when it's blanket bath time Matron.

MARK Come here, let's have a look.

MARK manipulates the knee- **PHIL** *winces.*

MARK How's that?

PHIL Better.

MARK Look- get these off.

I can't do anything-

PHIL *undoes and drops his trousers.*

MARK That's better-

Manipulates knee.

How's that?

PHIL Good-

PAUSE.

PHIL *puts his hand behind* **MARK***'s head and kisses him.*

PHIL Shit

Sorry-

I'll go and wait in the café.

MARK Look- can I ask you something-

PHIL No.

MARK Do you *want* to be with Patrick?

PHIL Why would you say that?

Of course I do.

Why do you think I'm stressing?

MARK I mean- okay your turn to tell me to mind my own business- the way you go on.

PHIL What way?

MARK 'You start with Heathcliff and you end up with Homer Simpson'

'You make your choices, there is no happy ever after'.

PHIL End of the day I want to be with him.

MARK You don't have sex.

PHIL So don't lots of people.

MARK And lots of people aren't happy.

Lots of people are in relationships- not **un**happy- but not happy either.

PHIL I want to be with Patrick-

Of course I do-

I'm feeling bad- no offence- because I've done something wrong-

MARK Or done something right?

PAUSE

Look at each other-

PHIL *is going to kiss him again.*

A horn outside

PHIL The AA man-

LIGHTS DOWN

SCENE SEVEN

A month later.

A primary school.

We can hear children singing Christmas songs-

PHIL *is wearing an elf costume.*

PHIL I'm not being funny

If anyone comes in-

You're the man giving a quote on new library shelves- Something like that.

Right-

We've 'Grandma got run over by a reindeer'-

And two choruses of 'Little Donkey.

Hi-

Good to see you.

You're looking well.

MARK Here-

MARK *hands him a scarf*

You dropped it.

PHIL Thanks-

You didn't have to.

MARK You dropped it when you ran away yesterday-

Pretending not to see me.

PHIL This really isn't such a good time-

MARK It never is-

PHIL Mistletoe and Wine

MARK *looks blank.*

PHIL The school Christmas Fayre-

Parents, kids and families.

MARK It's the one time knew I'd get to see you.

PHIL And you'd be happy if I turned up at your place of work?

MARK If you did-

You know what I'd say?

I say this is my friend Phil.

PAUSE

PHIL Look, I'm sorry I've not been in touch.

MARK It was you, wasn't it you bastard?

PHIL What?

Sorry?

Look- I've just been really busy-

We had OFSTED-

And then there was all that with Patrick.

MARK I only realised last night.

Like- 'duh'- how could have I been so thick-

I thought it was one of Michelle's mates.

PHIL I'm really not with you.

Look, like I say- I'm sorry I've been busy.

MARK People say that.

I mean how long does actually it take to send a text? An email even?

PHIL Look- Mark- you're going to have to explain this.

MARK When me and Michelle got back together-

PHIL Which is great by the way.

MARK If it's so great why did you run away from us yesterday?

PHIL It just- took me by surprise- seeing you both.

MARK What did you think I was going to do?

PHIL There were at least eight rolls of wallpaper in those bags-

That says to me there's something at stake.

MARK Michelle knows.

PHIL Sorry?

MARK I said she knows.

PHIL She knows-

MARK Michelle knows what happened.

PHIL With- us?

MARK Yes.

When we got back together- we did a lot of talking-

PHIL And you told her?

MARK Yes.

PHIL So- how was she about it?

MARK Surprised.

PHIL But okay?

MARK Not **not** okay.

PHIL Right.

MARK I take it you've not told Patrick?

Silly question.

PHIL Look, I really have got to go-

MARK You know why I got back with Michelle?

PHIL Because you want to be together?

MARK She'd been wanting to meet up.

And it was like I said to you-

I just couldn't see the point and all that.

And then she gets this anonymous letter-

'Mark's a smashing bloke'

'You two just need to get together'

We thought it must've been from one of her mates-

Saying basically 'you two are meant for each other, get your acts together'.

PHIL So you got back together.

MARK We had a big fuck off row …

But it made me think.

Made me realize – made us both realize-

All because of this letter

Which we thought it must've been from one of her mates-

Though they all denied it.

Then I saw you legging it yesterday.

You wrote that letter to Michelle.

PAUSE

PHIL It seemed the right thing to do.

Okay- maybe I shouldn't have done it//

MARK //No you shouldn't//

PHIL //but you're back together though. Bigger picture-

I know what I did- might seem a bit strange//

MARK //100%//

PHIL//but I could *see* you cared for her-

She wanted to see you-

And it just seemed like-

You were going to drift apart.

MARK It wasn't for you to do.

PHIL I'm sorry.

MARK And you dropped all communication.

PHIL It seemed…for the best.

MARK *turns to go- but stops and turns back.*

MARK You know what really gets me-

It's not so much that you did it-

But why you did it.

PHIL For you.

MARK If you were thinking of me you'd have replied to my texts-

Stayed in touch.

PHIL For you and for her.

MARK You see I don't buy that.

If I thought it was- but from where I'm standing-

Wasn't it was more for you?

PHIL No.

MARK That's what I think.

Get Mark safely back with Michelle-

Everything's nice and tidy again.

And guess what- I'm off the hook.

Back to my nice little life, which isn't that nice but what the heck.

PHIL That's truly not the case.

MARK After that weekend you dropped me like a fucking hot brick.

PHIL Okay- and I'm sorry.

But don't you think it was for the best?

MARK That's what people say when they wimp out. It's for the best.

PHIL Keep it down-

MARK What we had- it was weird-
It was random.

PHIL Exactly – at the end of the day-

Where was it going?

MARK Did it have to **go** anywhere?

What was it you said about zombie films?

Not putting a... *structure* on stuff-

Maybe it wasn't for me-

But it was for *me* to decide that-

Not for you to- tidy away.

PHIL Look, okay- things have been- difficult.

When I said about Patrick-

MARK What?

PAUSE

Is he okay?

PHIL He is now-

As long as he's sensible.

MARK What?

PHIL Long story short

He'd been off it for ages-

Temperatures, feeling generally crap-

One day he's just lying there spark out on the sofa-

Sarah comes round, takes one look at him and drags him off to A and E.

MARK And?

PHIL Late onset diabetes-

He's diabetic-

MARK So?

I mean that's okay- I mean it's not okay obviously- but it sort of is?

PHIL It's very livable with.

MARK I know a few people with it- My Auntie Linda…

PHIL It's all under control.

As I say he needs to be sensible- which he is being-

He's actually doing something about being healthy-

So it's not that particular apocalypse just yet. But – well, my focus needed to be at home.

MARK Right.

PHIL And so I thought- pretty much time to hang up the old walking boots.

MARK I'm sorry about Patrick//

PHIL //thanks//

MARK //But why didn't you tell me?

PHIL It didn't seem- right.

MARK Why?

PHIL I didn't want-

MARK -me to get the wrong idea?

PHIL Look- I'm sorry.

And now I really have got to go.
MARK What about meeting up sometime - for a drink?

PHIL I don't think it's a good idea.

MARK You know what Phil?

I look at you- you know what I see-

I see someone who's *scared* ...of life- of anything-

Anything different

'Better not do this'- how many times have I heard you say that-

'Better not this' 'Better go now'-

Why? Just what do you think is going to happen?

Scared choices

Okay- that's how you are-

But you know what?

I feel like I've been hung up with your fucking walking boots.

PHIL Let's not do this here-

MARK Where?

(Angry) Why not come round to ours?

Bring Patrick-

Michelle's been buying scatter cushions. We can talk about colour schemes. You can advise us on fucking floral borders. We can all have fucking pasta-

I don't really know what *us* was

But I tell you-

I know what it **wasn't**-

It wasn't a dirty little secret-

MARK *goes.*

LIGHTS DOWN

SCENE EIGHT

A chemo ward.

PHIL *is sat, hat on, with tubes in his arm.*

MARK *enters carrying a bag, looking around.*

PHIL Bloody hell.

MARK Hi there.

PHIL Bloody bloody hell.

MARK Shall I go out and come in again?

PHIL You're not-

You're not here for chemo?

MARK I'm here to see you, you daft prick.

If you don't want to chuck me out.

And I know it's been over a year-

And I'm sorry.

PHIL You've been busy?

MARK I've been a five star dick -

PHIL It's so good to see you.

MARK And I'm sorry about- last time.

PHIL I reckon I had it coming.

PAUSE

MARK How are you?

PHIL What, apart from the cancer?

MARK *looks horrified.*

Come on, laugh- everyone else does.

MARK You're doing okay?

PHIL I'm all right.

I mean we'll see what this lot all brings.

MARK It'll get rid of it?

PHIL Hard to say.

It's what you learn with cancer- nothing's clear-cut. Times, facts… cell counts… all fuzzy round the edges. It's a case of getting on with it.

But I'm good.

Gestures to the bag.

Not more clothes pegs?

MARK *Embarrassed* I'll show you later.

PHIL So- how did you even know I was here?

MARK Ah, well-

You're school came to the Centre didn't they-

And I'm like 'where's Mr. Middleton?'

So, of course they told me.

PHIL How did you know to come here?

MARK I went along to your house.

PHIL You've seen Patrick?

MARK He was at the gym.

There was some girl opened the door.

Seemed to be fitting a downstairs shower?

PHIL That'll be Sarah.

MARK I hope it's okay- me coming.

PHIL It's absolutely fine.

MARK And I hope it was okay me just poling up at the house.

PHIL That's fine too.

MARK Seriously?

PHIL Seriously.

It's so good to see you

PAUSE

They smile at each other.

MARK It's funny.

PHIL What is?

MARK You.

PHIL What part in particular? The tubes? The bald head?

MARK I just thought-

I just thought-

You'd be – you know-

All- stress on legs.

PHIL I have my moments.

MARK You just seem dead- chilled.

PHIL The thing is- if you spend your life scared of becoming ill-

When you **are** ill…

It's sort of like - there's nothing left to be scared of-

The Zombie Apocalypse has happened.

MARK I suppose.

PHIL You get to thinking about things-

Remember that time climbing Coniston Old Man?

MARK I certainly do.

PHIL That moment- when we got up to the top-
All- wet and knackered-

I think about it a lot.

It *mattered*.

And you look back- and you think-
There's things that matter- and things that don't.

MARK Okay-

PHIL You have your time- however long it may be-

And- like you always say-

It's **how** you use it-

You showed me that.

MARK I'll send you my bill.

I just can't get over how chilled you are.

PHIL They put something in the chemo, I think that helps.

Don't get me wrong- I have my moments-

After the last lot of chemo

Patrick and I- we went to Whitby.

MARK Nice.

PHIL Like we've always been saying- we should go- For years and years we've been saying it.

Every time I saw the weather pictures on Look North I'd think- I'd like to go there when I've got the time.

So one day- we **made** time- We just **went**.

And as we were driving there I thought-

Why did we never do this before?

And I was sat on this bench on the cliffs

Looking at the sea. The sun was starting to go down behind me.

There were these kids throwing a plastic Frisbee for a dog

And a trawler heading out to sea-

And I thought

There's *more* than just me.

It doesn't begin and end- with me. It…goes on. And I just got this feeling of…*peace.*

All those years I spent being scared-

Like you said- making scared choices-

And there's no need.

MARK Can I have some of what they put in your chemo?

They laugh.

PAUSE

Sarah said- the chances were- good?

PHIL They are.

MARK Good.

PHIL If you let yourself stare into that abyss- Face that apocalypse-

Not look away

And you let yourself…go there… it helps.

MARK But you're going to get well-

PHIL I know.

PAUSE

And you-

How's Gordale Scar?

MARK Still there.

PHIL The Centre?

MARK The usual ballus achus.

There's some Health and safety directive…

All zee harnesses

Ees not safe-Zo zee need zee replacements-
Total nightmare.

PHIL You're looking good.

MARK I need to take a leaf out of Patrick's book-
Get to the old gym a bit more.

PHIL You look fine

And Michelle-

You two good?

MARK We are.

PHIL All good on the scatter cushion front?

MARK There is something-

PHIL She's not sort of moved out?

MARK She's not sort of moved anything…

Not yet.

But in two weeks time-

All being well-

A sproglet is imminent.

PHIL Oh my God!

MARK Indeedy.

PHIL That's brilliant!

MARK Well I hope so-

PHIL So what happened?

MARK Well what d'you think?

PHIL I mean- presumably you talked?

MARK Not exactly-

Some cheap condoms from a machine in Ambleside.

PHIL Ah.

MARK Bit of the old shockeroonie.

PHIL I see.

MARK But then-

Well- I thought about your man-

You know- his two.

And I thought- well okay -

How hard can this be?

PHIL You can take him or her up Coniston Old Man.

MARK In a few years.

PHIL I'm going up again.

MARK Seriously?

PHIL Yes, absolutely seriously-

When this lot is over.

MARK On your own?

PHIL With Patrick-

The gym fit four-stone-less pounding that exercise bike Patrick-

Next stop- Climb Every Mountain for some new boots.

MARK So you're good?

PHIL We're good.

We faced that particular apocalypse too-

And surprise surprise- Realised we were where we wanted to be-with who we wanted to be with.

MARK Okay I didn't actually know I was going to do this-

PHIL What?

MARK *takes out a water pistol.*

PHIL Oh my God

Not-

MARK They didn't sell Chardonnay in the hospital shop-

So it's Vimto-

PHIL I like something fruity.

MARK Will you bloody well behave.

PHIL You're the one with a water pistol full of Vimto.

MARK Anyway- I better not-
It's a gesture.

PHIL Go on.

MARK D'you want me to get thrown out?

PHIL I'm a foul denizen of the undead remember-
Go on-

MARK *Fires water pistol into* **PHIL**'s *mouth.*

Nurse- I'm being attacked by a mad zombie killer-

PHIL *chokes.*

MARK *to an unseen nurse* I'm sorry- it's all right-

PHIL It's all down me-

MARK Come here.

MARK *wipes Phil's front and his mouth.*

A moment

PHIL So seen any good films?

MARK Yes, as a matter of fact- there's this new one out now- You must have heard of it.

PHIL Unlikely- unless it stars Mary Berry.

MARK War and Peace and Zombies.

PHIL Oh my God- Seriously?

MARK It's awesome.

PHIL You've seen this epic?

MARK Twice.

PHIL Go on then- spill-

MARK Well- it starts off on this battlefield- France and Russia-

And there's this Russian general-

PHIL Talking about the decline of the Russian aristocracy?

MARK No, having his leg sawn off-

Anyway… there's all this smoke drifting across the battlefield-

And these…figures come stumbling out of the smoke-

Lights dim as he recounts the film.

LIGHTS DOWN

NOTES FROM THE AUTHOR

As a writer one of the questions you're often asked is something along the lines of 'where do you get your ideas from?' The quick answer is both simple and complex; one likely to irritate and baffle in equal measure: ideas just come to you. Or rather they do to me.

A more considered answer is, of course, a bit more complex than that.

As someone who writes regularly (note I use the word 'regularly' as opposed to 'successfully') I'm always *always* on the lookout for ideas and am well used to viewing the daily discordant jangle of events and mentally assessing their as potential starting points for a story.

Working in a school as I do there's no shortage of those potential story starters. Conversations heard, arguments witnessed, crisis dealt with- plus the endless run of tales heard whilst queuing for the photocopier... And all the time there's a very cold, very detached part of my brain assessing and exploring those ideas- not by any real conscious effort on my part but because after thirty years it's something I'm in the habit of doing it- in the same way someone walking through a clothes shop will mentally try on the various outfits on display.

So the answer becomes not so much as where do I get my ideas, but how do I choose and develop the ideas that my mind relentlessly throws at me.

And again the answer is often both simple and complex.

Some ideas for whatever reason- for whatever chord they strike with whatever state my mind is in- just 'jump out'. Just as the person in the clothes shop sees a top or a shirt that instantly appeals- some ideas set off that same recognition, that feeling of 'I'm going to go with this'.

I don't really remember that exact moment with

'How to survive a zombie apocalypse'.

There was certainly a school outdoor residential in the mix, but also elements from the landscape of being in your fifties, that sense of time ticking- but really I can't be more precise than that.

The play is one play amongst the several I've written over the past ten to fifteen years, one idea amongst the many many I've chosen to explore (remember that caveat about writing regularly rather than successfully)

What made this particular play different was that thanks to the brilliant wonderful Manchester fringe and the efforts of all those involved- I had the chance stage it.

I'd like to thank in particular Lee, Toby, Andy, Matt and Emma, plus Lisa and the team at the Kings Arms and Mike from WriteForTheStage.

To me as a regular rather than successful writer that's the more interesting question: not where I get my ideas, but how in these days of arts austerity can writers get the chance to tell those stories that come to them.

J.H

ABOUT THE AUTHOR

Jonathan has writing credits that go back the best part of 30 years.

From humble beginnings - staging his own shows at The Bradford Playhouse - he's gone on to write for both the National Theatre and the Bush Theatre and has had numerous shows staged in London and at the Edinburgh Fringe (where he has twice won a prestigious Fringe First award.)

More recently he's had plays on in Bradford, Leeds, and Manchester and is currently working on shows for York Theatre Royal and the 2019 Manchester Fringe.

Amongst his many writing credits are Nativity (Edinburgh and Bradford), Behind the Aquarium at the Last Pizza Show (Edinburgh, Fringe First winner), Sweet As You Are (Y Touring, Edinburgh, Fringe First winner), The Midnight House (BBC R4), Flamingos (The Bush), The Coffee Lovers Guide To America (Chelsea Theatre), Juggling Chainsaws (National theatre studio), and last year's Manchester fringe winner How To Survive A Zombie Apocalypse.

He is co-chair of Script Yorkshire - an organisation that supports local writers - and is one of the lead figures in the growing Leeds Pub theatre scene.

And in amongst all of this, he somehow manages to work full time as Deputy Head of Primary School!

NOTES FROM THE PUBLISHER

Studio Salford has been around since 2003 and is a collective of in-house theatre companies producing new work in the intimate spaces at The Kings Arms Theatre, Salford. Through its productions, Development Week and development night *(Embryo)* many writers, actors and directors have learnt the ropes and have gone onto big things.

Mike Heath runs the *Studio Salford WriteForTheStage* (WFTS) courses. Work produced through the courses have gone on to full productions with (and without) support from Arts Council England. Participant writers have gone onto to full rural touring of subsequent work and publication of novels.

WFTS is based at The Kings Arms, Salford but is also available for distance learning. Details of the course can be found at **www.writeforthestage.co.uk**

WriteForTheStage Books is the publishing arm of the WFTS courses. The aim is to help sustain the life of the work produced through the course once the course has been completed. More information is available on the website.

PERFORM THIS PLAY

The following rights are available for this play:

Professional Rights

Amateur Rights

Fringe Rights

Educational Rights

To find out how to get the rights to perform this play in part or in full, please email **info@writeforthestage.co.uk**

BE A PLAYWRIGHT

Do you dream of seeing your writing on stage, performed by professional actors and in front of an audience? Maybe you don't know where to start.

The *Studio Salford WriteForTheStage* courses cater for total beginners, learning the fundamentals of story-telling for the stage, to more experienced writers who require guidance and dramaturgy support. We aim to support writers from a diverse background, and those who are excluded from Young Writers Schemes.

WriteForTheStage is an affordable means of learning and developing your skills. Based in Salford, Greater Manchester, Glossop, and online, there's a course that will help you discover the next stage of your career.

See **www.writeforthestage.co.uk** for more details.

Printed in Great Britain
by Amazon